The Water Caller

Sean McCollum   Illustrated by Peter Scanlan

STECK-VAUGHN
Harcourt Supplemental Publishers

www.steck-vaughn.com

ISBN 0-7398-7529-9

Power Up! Building Reading Strength is a trademark of
Steck-Vaughn.

Printed in China.

1 2 3 4 5 6 7 8 9 M 07 06 05 04 03

Contents

CHAPTER 1
The Colony

"Do you two have enough water?" Luna asked. She always asked that question, even if she and her friends were just walking to the dining hall.

Kirian raised the water bottle hanging from his shoulder and nodded.

Luna turned to Rayna. "What about you?"

"I don't need it," Rayna said. "We're just going to the *Mayflower*. It's only a mile away, so stop worrying."

Rayna knew they should worry, though. No rain had fallen on the planet in nine months. Their people were running out of water.

The three friends walked up and down some small hills. Rubbery silver gummi-grass bent with the wind. The planet's sun was bright in the red sky.

A short time later, the *Mayflower* loomed in front of the three friends. In the year 2506, the huge ship had brought two hundred people from Earth to start a colony on Alphus, a dry planet with three moons. The ship had a rough landing. Twelve years later, the *Mayflower* was still grounded.

"We always knew this might be a one-way trip," Rayna's dad often said.

Commander Trig Royce was Rayna's father and the leader of the New Jamestown colony. For weeks, his workers had been drilling for underground water all day and all night. They were almost out of the oil they needed to run their machines. Commander Royce had sent his daughter and her two friends to get more oil from the *Mayflower*. ⚡

The friends finally reached the main door of the *Mayflower*. Rayna pushed three buttons to open it. They went inside and grabbed some heavy bottles of brown oil.

As they walked away from the ship, Kirian looked sad. "Can we stop by the cemetery on the way home?" he asked softly.

Luna put a hand on his shoulder. "Are you sure you'll be okay?" she asked. Luna was like a sister to Kirian. He had moved in with Luna's family after his parents had died.

Kirian nodded, and the friends headed toward the cemetery. It was on a small hill about halfway between New Jamestown and the *Mayflower*. Rows of orange stones marked all the places where colonists were buried.

Most of the people had died from a strange disease during the colony's first year. The Sickness had killed nearly a hundred of them.

Kirian visited the spot where both of his parents were buried. Luna stood in front of the stone of her older sister. Rayna quickly found the marker she was looking for. She read the words on the stone: *Alyssa Royce—died 2506*. Rayna had seen pictures of her mother, but she had been too young to have many memories of Alyssa Royce.

As they stood in the cemetery, the friends heard strange voices. "*Hoo-bah, hoo-bah, hoo-bah.*"

Rayna and Luna looked up at the same time. The voices were coming from the other side of the hill. "What is that?" Luna asked.

Kirian stared at the ground and walked up the hill. He seemed to be following something. Then he turned around and pointed down.

"The Alphans are here," he said.

Luna and Rayna looked surprised. They joined Kirian and stared at the soil. He had been following a set of footprints.

The Alphans were creatures that had lived on Alphus for a long time—long before the colonists had landed. Most colonists thought that the Alphans were primitive because they didn't use machines. The colonists didn't know much about them. That was because humans and Alphans spoke very different languages and hadn't spent much time together. The creatures lived in the hills and rarely came near New Jamestown.

"Hoo-bah, HOO-bah, HOO-BAH." The voices grew louder. They seemed to beat from inside Rayna's chest. The sound pulled her toward the top of the hill, where the footprints led. Kirian and Luna followed.

"Where are you going?" Luna whispered. "We don't know whether they're dangerous!"

"Dad told me that the Alphans have never hurt anyone," Rayna replied.

"They haven't hurt anyone *yet*," Kirian said.

"Have you ever seen one of them, Rayna?" Luna asked.

"I've only seen them from far away," Rayna answered.

"They're very weird," Kirian said softly. "I saw them up close once. They eat gummi-grass and make strange noises."

The friends crawled to the top of the hill on their hands and knees and peeked over it. At the bottom of the hill, seven Alphans were moving in a big circle. Their large bodies were covered with short, silver fur. Each creature was the size of a bear.

The Alphans each held a rope as the group circled. The ropes led to a ten-foot-tall tube standing in the center of their circle. Rayna thought that the tube looked like a big rubber hose woven out of gummi-grass.

Smaller hoses came out of the top of the tube. There was a gummi-grass bag at the end of each small hose. The Alphans sang *"hoo-bah"* as they circled, turning the large tube with the ropes.

"They're so weird," said Kirian again, under his breath.

"Check out the sparkling blue pool under them," Rayna whispered. "It looks like they're walking on water."

Luna glanced at Kirian, then at Rayna. "What blue pool?" Luna asked.

Rayna gave her a strange look. "It's right under them," she said. "Can't you see it?"

"No," said Luna. "Come on, it's just dirt."

Rayna was shocked. The blue pool was as clear to her as the sun above. "It's right there!" she insisted loudly.

The Alphans stopped circling. Two of them looked up at the humans.

"Uh-oh," Kirian said.

One of the Alphans pointed at the three friends and hummed loudly in its language. *"Look at those young Sky Fallers!"* it said.

Rayna stood up to run, but something stopped her. She had understood exactly what the creature had said! No colonist had ever been able to understand the Alphan language.

All the Alphans were humming now. The sound made Rayna dizzy. She lost her balance and fell. Kirian and Luna reached for her, but it was too late. Rayna rolled down the hill toward the Alphans.

As she tumbled, pictures flashed in her head. She saw a crying child, a pair of hands, and a woman with black hair.

Rayna rolled to a stop at the bottom of the hill. Then she heard a voice say, *"Hum-oh! This is big trouble."* That was the last thing she remembered.

Kirian and Luna watched in shock as the Alphans surrounded Rayna. One Alphan started to climb the hill toward the two friends. Luna turned to run. Kirian didn't move. He stared down at Rayna.

"Let's go!" Luna yelled. "We'll get help and come back!" Kirian finally turned around. The two of them raced over the hill, away from the Alphan climbing toward them.

On the outer edge of New Jamestown, Trig Royce sat in his work tent. Bexer, Luna's dad, stood beside him. Bexer was one of the drill workers. The two men stared at a map on Trig's computer. The roar of the drill outside made it hard for them to think.

"This doesn't make any sense," Trig said.

"What's that, Commander Royce?" asked Bossa Mabb, standing at the door of the tent. She was the colony's chief security officer. Bossa was tall and strong, with brown hair.

"Good morning, Officer Mabb," said Trig. He looked up quickly, then looked back at his computer.

Bexer said, "Our tests show that there's water below this spot. The water disappears when our drill gets close to it, though."

"I don't get it," Trig said softly.

"Well, you'd better get it soon, sir," Bossa said. She sat on the edge of his desk. "We only have enough water for one more month."

Trig sat back and folded his arms. "Yes, we already know that, Bossa."

"The colonists are losing confidence in you, Commander," she said.

Trig gave her a tired smile. "You think you and Tyrus could do a better job, don't you?" Tyrus Mabb was Bossa's husband. He was also a security officer.

Before she could answer, Bossa was startled by the sound of running feet outside. Kirian and Luna nearly tripped as they ran into the tent, breathing hard.

Bexer ran around the desk to his daughter. "What's going on, Luna?" he asked.

Luna tried to catch her breath as she spoke. "The Alphans . . . have got . . . Rayna!"

Trig quickly called a rescue team together, including Tyrus Mabb. Bossa gave each team member a shock-stick.

Then Bossa looked at Kirian and Luna. "Where did you see the Alphans?" she asked.

Trig tapped Bossa on the shoulder and pointed to a hill near the tent. "It doesn't matter. They've come to us. Look."

Five Alphans were standing on the hill. One of them was carrying Rayna.

"We'll get her, Trig. Don't worry," Bossa said quietly. She turned to Tyrus. "Get behind those creatures."

Trig raised his hand. "Wait. The Alphans have never hurt anyone. Give me a minute."

He walked up the hill toward the creatures. As he got closer, the tall Alphan laid Rayna gently on the ground. Then it backed away. Rayna sat up slowly and rubbed her eyes.

Trig knelt down beside his daughter. "Are you okay?" he asked Rayna.

"Yes," Rayna answered, blinking. "I'm just a little dizzy."

Trig slowly walked toward the Alphans and looked closely at them. Each Alphan had a rubbery bag hanging from one shoulder.

"Thank you," Trig said. The tall Alphan answered him with soft humming.

Trig shook his head. "I wish I knew what you were saying."

"It said that it's glad to see you again," Rayna answered. Then she looked puzzled. "It also asked if I was 'the one.'"

Trig turned to his daughter with a startled look. Then he heard Bossa behind him. She had followed him up the hill.

"You mean you can understand these stupid beasts?" growled Bossa.

Before Rayna could answer, angry voices came from below. Four Alphans had seen the big drilling machine and were moving toward it. They were making loud humming noises, as if they were upset. One Alphan was pounding the ground with its fists.

Tyrus ran toward the four creatures. He pointed his shock-stick at one of them. A bolt of electricity struck the Alphan, and it fell, dropping the rubbery sack that hung from its shoulder. The other three Alphans backed away from Tyrus.

After a minute, the shocked Alphan got up. It stumbled to the other three, and the group moved to where Rayna was sitting on the ground. The tall Alphan hummed to Rayna.

"The Alphan says we're harming the land with our drill," Rayna said. "It says we're doing terrible things to this planet."

"Tell it that we'll do terrible things to its people if they don't get out of here," Bossa said. She gave Rayna a nasty look. Then she

raised her shock-stick and took a step toward the Alphans. Trig blocked her path.

"Get out of the way, Commander," said Bossa. "This is my job. We can't trust them."

Rayna got to her feet slowly. *"You should go,"* she hummed to the Alphans in their language.

The tall Alphan took a step forward. It hummed back to Rayna, *"If you do not listen, you will all die soon. We wish to help. You know this is true."*

Rayna turned and saw more colonists coming up the hill. They carried shock-sticks.

"Go!" Rayna repeated. The tall Alphan backed off and hummed to the other Alphans. They all turned and hurried away.

Bossa glared at Rayna. "Maybe it's you we can't trust," Bossa said.

Trig put an arm around his daughter to help her walk. As they headed home, Rayna felt all the colonists watching her. ⚡

CHAPTER 3

Discoveries

"This is too weird," Rayna said, her hand covering her eyes. She lay on her sleeping mat on the floor. "Why can I suddenly understand what the Alphans are saying?"

Trig paced through the hut. Then he looked at Rayna and sighed. "Something happened to you when you were a baby," he said. "It was during the colony's first year."

"You mean during the Sickness?"

"Yes. I never told you about it because I didn't think it had changed anything in you." He stopped pacing and smiled. "I guess it did."

"It turned me into a freak, whatever it was," Rayna said under her breath.

"It saved your life," Trig insisted. He sat down on a supply box next to Rayna. "Half of the colony was about to die from the disease. You and your mom were the last ones to get sick." Trig's eyes shone with tears.

He reached over and lifted a photograph off his desk. It was a picture from thirteen years before. He handed it to Rayna.

In the picture, Alyssa Royce was wearing a doctor's coat. Rayna realized that she had seen her mom's face in her mind when she had fallen down the hill.

"Your mom had been trying to find a cure for months. In the end, she came up with one last plan to save your life," Trig continued.

"One night, I drove around with the two of you in search of the Alphans," Rayna's dad said. "We met a small group of them near the *Mayflower*. They looked afraid as we got close to them, but your mother was able to make them feel calm. She wanted to get some of their blood, but she knew that they'd be afraid.

"First, she showed the Alphans how sick you were. Then, she took some blood from my arm to show them that her needle wouldn't harm them. At last, one of the Alphans held

out one of its arms, and your mother took some of its silver blood."

"Was it the tall Alphan that said it was glad to see you again?" Rayna asked.

"I think so," Trig answered. "Your mother used its blood to make the medicine that saved you. There was only enough for you, though. She died before she could make more."

"That's why it called me 'the one,'" Rayna said. "Why would the medicine give me the power to speak Alphan?"

"You're not a little girl anymore," Trig replied. He ran his hand over Rayna's hair. "I think some of the Alphans' powers are showing up in you as you grow older."

Rayna sat up. Her eyes were full of fear. "Are you saying that I'm part Alphan?"

Trig sighed. "Well, you could say that. I never told anyone because people might have been frightened. Some colonists still think that the Alphans are very strange—even dangerous."

Suddenly, there was a loud pounding on the door of the hut. Trig stood up quickly, but Bossa pushed her way inside before he could invite her in. Tyrus followed behind her. He held up a rubbery sack in a gummi-grass basket. It was the sack that the Alphan had dropped by the drilling machine.

"What's going on?" Trig asked.

"You tell us," Bossa growled. She raised the sack and squeezed it. Water dripped slowly into her mouth.

"It's water," Tyrus said. "The Alphans have water, and I bet your Alphan-loving daughter knows where they got it."

"I'm not sure where they got it," insisted Rayna. She told the Mabbs everything she remembered about her time with the Alphans.

Bossa folded her arms. "What about your sudden gift for speaking their language?"

Rayna hesitated and looked at her dad. He gave a small shake of his head to tell her not to say anything. "I don't know," Rayna lied.

"I think you're lying," Tyrus said.

"That's enough from both of you," Trig said loudly. He marched to the door and opened it. "Get out."

Tyrus left with the water sack. Bossa paused in the doorway. "We'll all be dead in a month if we don't get water, Commander," she said. "It's my duty to save us, since you can't."

Trig slammed the door behind her. Rayna sighed with relief. "Why is Bossa so mad at us?" she asked.

"She and Tyrus had a daughter the same age as you," her father answered. "She died from the Sickness. I think seeing you upsets them. They don't understand why you lived and she didn't."

The next day at school, no one talked to Rayna. When she sat down in art class, other students sitting nearby moved away. She bit her lip to hold back tears. It was bad enough that her dad had told her she was part Alphan. Now no one wanted to be her friend.

At lunch, Rayna joined Luna and Kirian at a table. Luna tapped her feet nervously. When Rayna offered to share her Nut-Nut protein bar with Kirian, he shook his head.

"What's going on?" Rayna asked with a smile. "You never say no to a Nut-Nut protein bar, Kirian." Both Kirian and Luna were quiet.

"Are the rumors true?" Luna finally asked.

"Are what rumors true?" Rayna said.

"Can you really talk with Alphans? Do you really know where there's water?"

Rayna tried to joke with her friend. "None of it's true. I'm just a sweet, human girl."

"Bossa Mabb says it's true," Luna snapped.

"Bossa just wants my dad's job," Rayna shot back at her.

"Some people say she should take his job," Kirian said quietly. "He isn't finding water."

Rayna dropped her protein bar and got up from her seat. "You would believe her over me, wouldn't you?" She glared at Luna, who looked down. "What great friends you are!" Rayna turned to walk away.

"My dad said we're not even supposed to talk to you!" Luna said loudly.

"You're a freak," Kirian added.

Kirian's words hit Rayna like a shock-stick. Tears boiled in her eyes. She wanted to shout something back. Instead, she shook with anger.

After taking a deep breath, she found the words she wanted to say. "Don't talk about my father. In fact, don't ever talk to me again."

As she marched away, Rayna started to feel something besides anger. She felt lonely. Her best friends had turned against her.

CHAPTER 4
Night Journey

That night, Rayna couldn't sleep at all. She listened to the wind rattle the sides of the hut. She thought about her dad, who was working at the drill site with his crew.

Rayna was sure they wouldn't find any sources of water. She also knew that a supply ship from Earth would never reach them in time. "We're all alone," Rayna said in the darkness. Without thinking, she hummed in the Alphan language, *"I'm all alone."*

"No, you are not," hummed another voice. Rayna sat up. A cold chill ran down her back. Two sets of Alphan eyes were watching her from just inside the hut's door.

Two large Alphans had squeezed inside the hut. They smelled fresh, like gummi-grass wet with rain. *"Rayna, do not be afraid,"* hummed one of them. It was the tall one, the one that had given its blood for her.

"I am Ba-Hoom. This is Mor-Mar. There is something we must show you now. Come with us, please."

Rayna hesitated. She was scared to go into the night with the two Alphans. She knew the Alphans were taking a big chance by coming to her hut, though. Whatever they wanted to show her must be important.

She quickly put on her boots and followed the Alphans outside. It was after midnight, so no one was in the streets. The three trotted out of New Jamestown and into the hills.

As they ran, Ba-Hoom pointed to the three bright moons above them. *"When the moons are together like this, the rains stop."*

Rayna thought about how long the planet had been without rain. *"That's right,"* she replied. *"It hasn't rained for nine months, since the moons started appearing together."*

"During this time, the rains stop for three years," Ba-Hoom continued. *"You Sky Fallers must learn this."*

"Where do you find water when the rains stop?" Rayna hummed.

"You will see," Ba-Hoom replied. The three kept climbing through the hills.

"You call my people 'Sky Fallers,'" said Rayna as they walked. *"What do you call your people?"*

"We are 'Water Callers,'" said Mor-Mar.

They reached the edge of a gully. Mor-Mar paused. *"Do you hear something?"*

Rayna heard engines. *"It's our drill. We use it to find water,"* she told the Alphans.

"*Let us show you how to find water the right way,*" said Ba-Hoom. He pointed to the gully below. There Rayna saw the strange, sparkling blue pool she had seen before. Five Alphans stood around it. One was carrying a large rubbery tube woven of gummi-grass.

"*Do you see it?*" Ba-Hoom asked.

"Yes. That's water?"

"The blue pool shows us where there is underground water," explained Mor-Mar. "If you dig and tear at the land for it, the water will flow away. We Water Callers know how to bring it to the surface."

The three of them climbed down into the gully. Rayna watched as the Alphans set the tube into the center of the blue pool. They attached water sacks to the hanging hoses.

Then the Alphans picked up the long ropes attached to the middle of the tube. With a signal from Ba-Hoom, they moved in a circle. They sang "hoo-bah, hoo-bah" as they sped up.

After a few minutes, Rayna heard gurgling in the tube. Then the water sacks shook. She could tell that they were filling with water.

"Would you like to help?" Mor-Mar asked.

"Sure!" said Rayna. She joined Mor-Mar on a rope.

"You see, we must be gentle. The more you use your machines, the farther the water flows away," Mor-Mar said. *"Even we are having trouble finding sources of water now."*

Suddenly, bright lights swirled around Rayna and the Alphans. Creepjeeps raced into the gully, raising clouds of dust. Rayna knew right away that Bossa Mabb had followed her.

Colonists jumped out of the creepjeeps and pointed their shock-sticks at the Alphans. The creatures backed away, humming in alarm. The Alphans—and Rayna—were trapped.

Rayna raised a hand to protect her eyes from the bright lights. She saw Bossa marching toward her.

Bossa pointed at the sacks of water and said, "I knew you were lying. You knew where to find water all along." She waved to one of the colonists. It was Bexer, Luna's dad. "Lock Rayna up. Then drive the drilling machine back here. Don't forget, Bexer, I'm in charge now."

Bossa grabbed Rayna's arm and led her to Bexer's creepjeep.

Bexer drove the creepjeep toward his hut. Rayna saw a light go on inside as Bexer turned off the engine. Then she saw Luna and Kirian watching her through a window. She felt scared and embarrassed at the same time.

"I'm sorry," Bexer said, helping her out of the creepjeep. "I have to do my duty."

In the moonlight, his sad eyes showed that he didn't like what he was doing. Bexer led her to the back of his hut and unlocked a shed. He pointed for Rayna to go inside. "We've never needed a jail before. This is the best I can do," he said.

He locked the door behind Rayna. A minute later, the creepjeep sped away. Rayna felt her way around the dark shed.

"Mm-mm!" The sound startled her. Then she realized that it was her dad's voice. She found him on the floor and pulled a piece of cloth away from his mouth.

"Hello, Rayna," he said, trying to sound cheerful. "We're in quite a mess, aren't we?"

CHAPTER 5

The Water Caller

Rayna untied her dad's hands. She sat on the dirt floor and put her head in her hands.

"I led Bossa right to the Alphans," Rayna said. "This is all my fault." She heard her father moving in the darkness. "Are you listening to me, Dad?"

"Yes, I'm just looking for a way out. We might still have a chance to stop Bossa from hurting the Alphans." Trig paused. "This is not your fault, Rayna. We're all afraid because we're running out of water. Fear makes people do things they usually wouldn't do."

"Bossa seems to enjoy scaring people," said Rayna with a sigh.

Trig moved closer to his daughter. "Don't be too hard on Bossa," he said. "I don't like what she's doing, either, but I've worked with her for years. She can be a good officer."

Then they heard the sound of footsteps. "Someone's coming," whispered Trig.

"Rayna?" Luna's voice called from the other side of the wall.

"Hi, Luna," replied Rayna in a low voice. She knew Luna and Kirian had watched her get locked up. She still felt angry at them. "Do you want to laugh and call me a freak again?"

"No," said Luna. "We're sorry. You've been too good a friend for us to be so nasty."

"We'll make it up to you," Kirian said.

Their answers surprised Rayna. Her anger went away. She was quiet for a minute as she felt her way to the door.

"I'm sorry, too," Rayna finally said. "I didn't tell you the whole truth. The great thing is, we can all make it up to each other now. We just have to trust each other like never before."

Luna moaned. "You're going to get us into big trouble, aren't you?"

Rayna smiled. Then Trig spoke. "Just get us out of here if you can."

Rayna heard Kirian mumble something and then trot away.

"Kirian says that he knows where a key is," Luna said.

Bossa Mabb's face burned with anger. Bexer had driven the drilling machine from town. He and the colonists were using it to dig at the site where the Alphans had gotten water. The drill had found nothing but sand, though.

Bossa picked up a shock-stick and marched toward the Alphans. She used the stick to draw a picture of an Alphan in the sand.

"You'll show us how to get water, or you'll get this," Bossa said calmly. She struck the drawing with the shock-stick, and sparks flew. Ba-Hoom stepped forward, humming.

"Show us!" Bossa shouted with fury. She pointed the shock-stick at the tall Alphan. Tyrus came and stood beside her.

A voice called from above. "Ba-Hoom says they will not help you!"

Surprised, Bossa looked up.

Rayna stared down at Bossa from the edge of the gully. Trig, Kirian, and Luna stood beside Rayna. "They don't respect you, Bossa. Ba-Hoom says that you only know how to grab, not how to give!" Rayna said.

"Rayna, I'm so glad you came back," Bossa said coldly, trying to stay calm. "Now we can finally talk with these monsters."

Rayna scrambled down the wall of the gully. "We're not monsters, Officer Mabb," Rayna said, loudly enough for all of the colonists to hear her.

"What do you mean, 'we'?" Bossa tried to joke. "You don't look like some primitive Alphan, Rayna."

Rayna saw her chance. She turned to all the colonists. "Isn't Alphus our home?" she asked. Her voice echoed in the gully. "Won't we live the rest of our lives here and be buried here?" She paused. "Aren't we all Alphans now?"

Rayna continued before Bossa could stop her. "Here's the deal. If we can bring water from the ground here, Bossa Mabb must step down as leader!" She pointed to the Alphans. "If we respect this planet and its creatures, there will be water for everyone."

The colonists all started talking and mumbling. Bexer climbed down from the drilling machine.

"Can you really show us how we can get water?" he asked.

"Yes," Rayna said.

Bexer stared at Bossa for a moment. Then he turned to the other colonists and shouted, "What do we have to lose?"

Bossa's face turned red with fury. She walked to the nearest creepjeep and threw her shock-stick in the back.

"Go for it, Rayna!" Kirian and Luna yelled from the edge of the gully.

Rayna hummed to Ba-Hoom. *"Can we still get the water?"* Earlier, the sparkling blue pool had been large. Now it looked small and dim.

Ba-Hoom hummed back. *"I do not know. Much of the water has flowed away because of the drilling. We must hurry."*

The Alphans brought out the gummi-grass tube. Each creature took a rope. Rayna joined Mor-Mar. They began moving in a circle. Around they went, faster and faster, singing *"hoo-bah."*

Rayna waited for the gurgle of water in the tube. Nothing happened. She was losing confidence. Rayna felt like her heart would burst if they failed.

"Faster!" Ba-Hoom hummed. The Alphans were slowly getting exhausted, though.

Then something wonderful happened. Rayna saw her father join the circle, taking a rope from a tired Alphan. Bexer grabbed a rope from another Alphan. Luna and Kirian scrambled into the group to help out, too. *"Hoo-bah! Hoo-bah! Hoo-bah!"* the colonists sang. The circle turned faster.

Finally, the water came. At first, Rayna thought she was imagining it. Then the tube gurgled. The water sacks began to fill.

A huge cheer went up from the colonists, and they gathered around the circle. Rayna was laughing and crying at the same time.

Later, Rayna sat on the ground with Luna, Kirian, and Ba-Hoom. She was exhausted and wet, but she was also happier than she could ever remember being. She no longer felt alone or afraid.

"Don't look now, but here comes Bossa," Luna said under her breath.

Bossa walked toward Rayna and knelt beside her. Bossa looked as though she'd been crying. "This is not easy for me to say, Rayna. I am very, very sorry. I thought I was doing what had to be done. I felt so afraid—afraid we would die."

Rayna reached out and took Bossa's hand. "There's been enough fear around here," said Rayna. "We're going to be okay. We're all Alphans now."

To Rayna's shock, even Bossa and Tyrus Mabb jumped into the swirling mix of humans and Alphans. When the sacks were full, water shot from cracks in the tube. Everyone danced in the spraying water.